Dairy Farming

by Grace Hansen

Abdo Kids Jumbo is an Imprint of Abdo Kids
abdobooks.com

abdobooks.com

Published by Abdo Kids, a division of ABDO, P.O. Box 398166, Minneapolis, Minnesota 55439.
Copyright © 2024 by Abdo Consulting Group, Inc. International copyrights reserved in all countries.
No part of this book may be reproduced in any form without written permission from the publisher.
Abdo Kids Jumbo™ is a trademark and logo of Abdo Kids.

Printed in the United States of America, North Mankato, Minnesota.

052023

092023

THIS BOOK CONTAINS
RECYCLED MATERIALS

Photo Credits: AP Images, Getty Images, Shutterstock, United States Department of Agriculture

Production Contributors: Teddy Borth, Jennie Forsberg, Grace Hansen
Design Contributors: Victoria Bates, Candice Keimig

Library of Congress Control Number: 2022946720
Publisher's Cataloging-in-Publication Data

Names: Hansen, Grace, author.

Title: Dairy farming / by Grace Hansen

Description: Minneapolis, Minnesota : Abdo Kids, 2024 | Series: Agriculture in the USA! | Includes online
    resources and index.

Identifiers: ISBN 9781098266196 (lib. bdg.) | ISBN 9781098266899 (ebook) | ISBN 9781098267247
    (Read-to-me ebook)

Subjects: LCSH: Dairy manufacture--Juvenile literature. | Agriculture--Juvenile literature. | Dairy farming--
    Juvenile literature. | Dairy products--Juvenile literature.

Classification: DDC 637.1--dc23

Table of Contents

Dairy Farms

More than 40,000 dairy farms can be found throughout the United States. These farms raise dairy cows. Dairy cows produce milk.

The dairy **industry** creates around 900,000 jobs in the US. The largest milk-producing states are California, Wisconsin, Idaho, New York, and Texas.

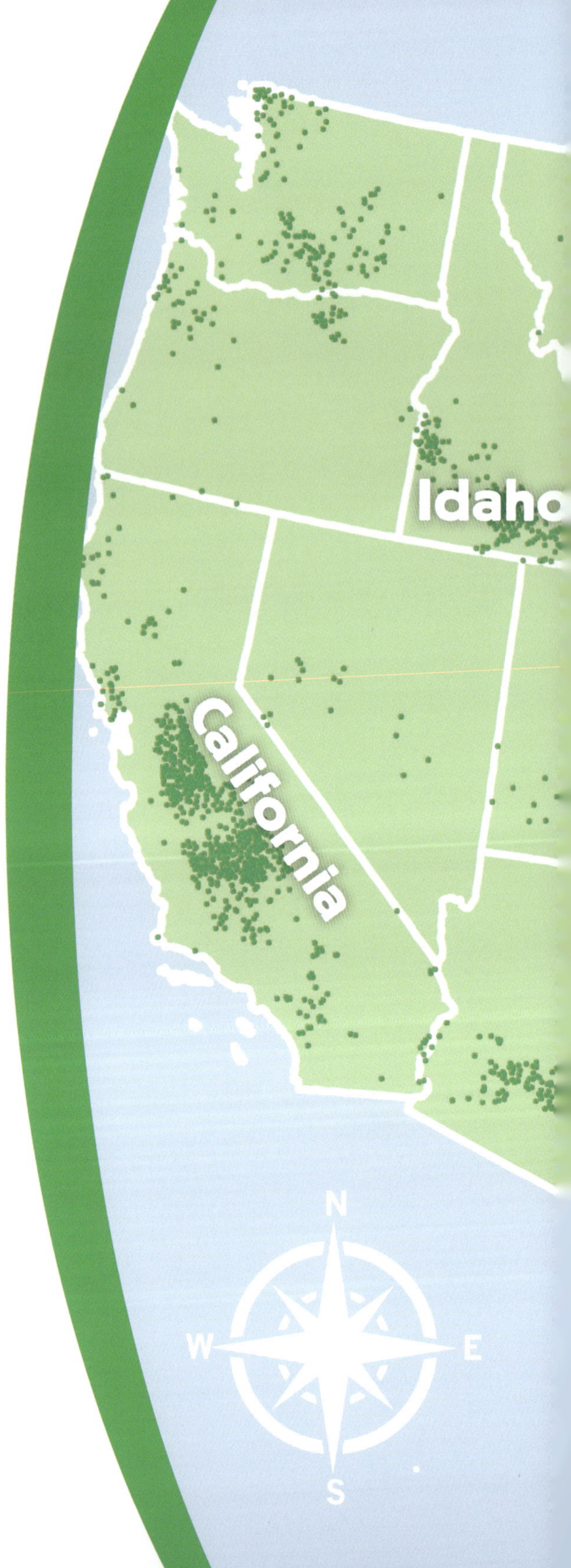

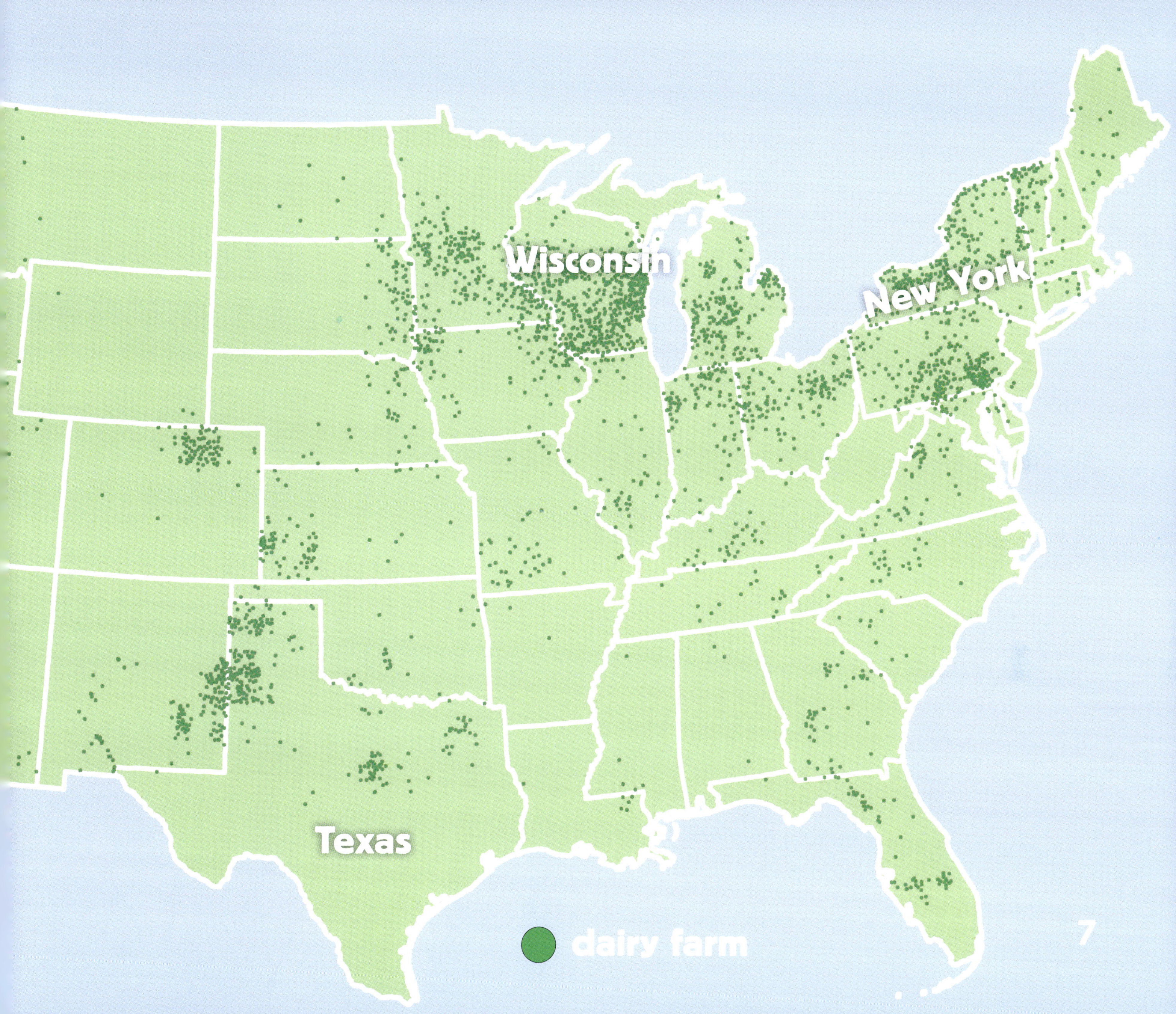

Wisconsin
New York
Texas
dairy farm

Most dairy farms in the United States are family owned. These farmers are experts in dairy cow care and milk production.

Happy Cows

Dairy cows are well cared for. They are fed a healthy diet and given fresh water each day. They are sheltered from the heat and cold. Happy cows make good milk!

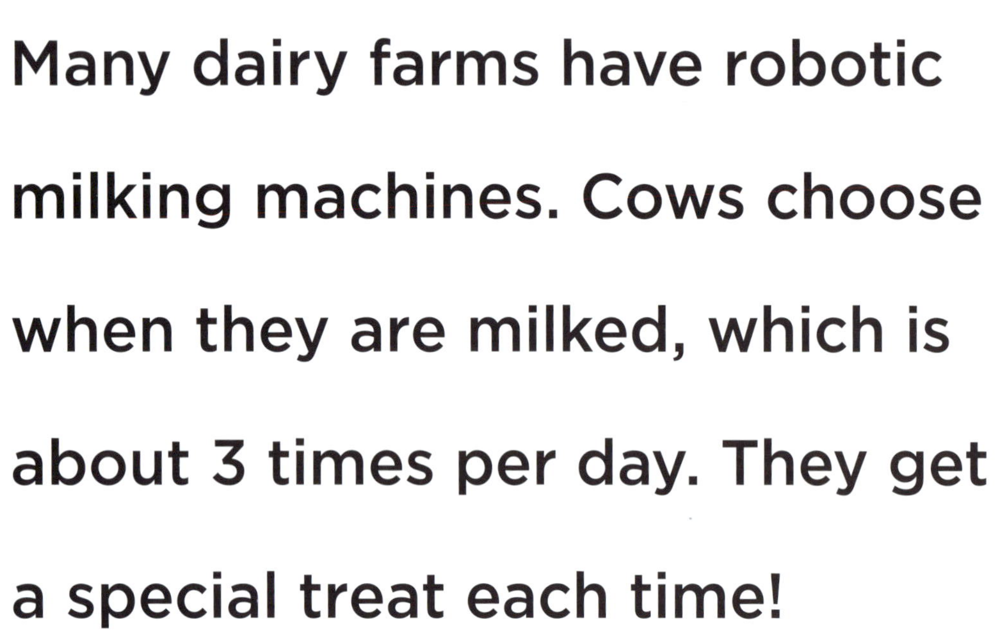

Many dairy farms have robotic milking machines. Cows choose when they are milked, which is about 3 times per day. They get a special treat each time!

EMERGENCY STOP

Dairy Cow to Table

The milk is tested for safety. Tanker trucks that haul milk visit the farm at least once a day. The trucks take the milk to a processing plant.

Fonterra
Dairy for life
Fonterra
Dairy for life
SCANIA
R 580
382
LLK826

The milk is tested again at the plant. This is to make sure the milk is safe and pure. Then it is **pasteurized** and **homogenized**.

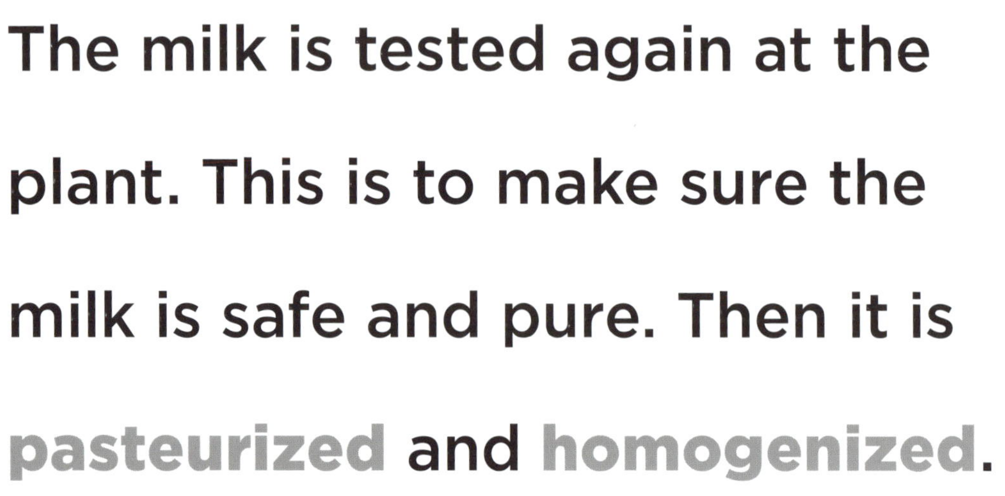

eedom evo
54185

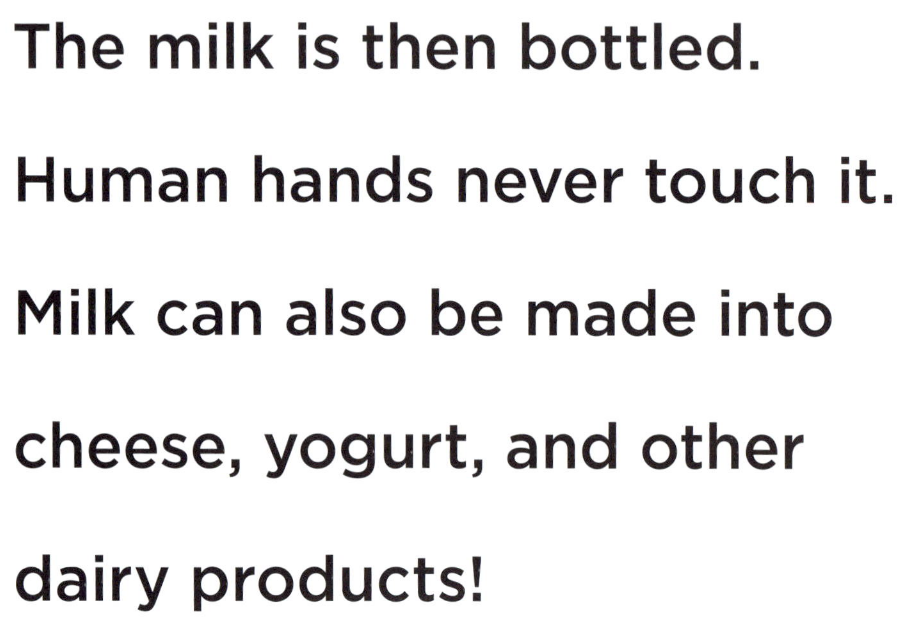

The milk is then bottled.
Human hands never touch it.
Milk can also be made into
cheese, yogurt, and other
dairy products!

Milk and milk products are then delivered to grocery stores. Grocery stores keep everything fresh and cold.

Hilltop
Fresh Creamy
Dairy

Common Dairy Cow Breeds

Holstein Cow

- Known for its black-and-white spotted body
- **Originated** in the Netherlands

- Brought to the United States in the 1850s

Jersey Cow

- Known for its large eyes and brown color
- Its milk is high in butterfat and perfect for making ice cream
- Came from the island of Jersey, a country in the English Channel near France

Glossary

homogenized – processed to break up and blend in the particles of fat.

industry – a number of companies making a particular product.

originated – came from or began to exist.

pasteurized – heated for a certain length of time to kill any harmful bacteria.

Index

Abdo Kids
ONLINE
FREE! ONLINE MULTIMEDIA RESOURCES

Visit **abdokids.com** to access crafts, games, videos, and more!

Use Abdo Kids code
ADK6196
or scan this QR code!